quick and easy

pizzas
and pasta

Food & Styling DONNA HAY
Photography QUENTIN BACON

TRIDENT
PRESS
INTERNATIONAL

Introduction

In this book you will find a host of recipes for two of the world's favourite foods - pizzas and pasta. Packed with mouthwatering recipes for these ever-popular foods, this book will become an invaluable kitchen companion to today's cook.

You will be surprised at the variety of pizzas you can create in your own kitchen - individual pizzas that are ideal finger and picnic food, or large round or rectangular pizzas suitable for feeding a team of hungry teenagers, or those wonderful filled pizzas called calzone. The pasta recipes are just as exciting and you will find ideas and recipes suitable for easy entertaining, family meals, the health-conscious and vegetarians.

Published by:
TRIDENT PRESS INTERNATIONAL
801 12th Avenue South
Suite 302
Naples, FL 34102 U.S.A.
(c)Trident Press
Tel: (941) 649 7077
Fax: (941) 649 5832
Email: tridentpress@worldnet.att.net
Website: www.trident-international.com

Quick & Easy Pizzas and Pasta

EDITORIAL
Food Editor: Rachel Blackmore
Editorial and Production Assistant: Sheridan Packer
Editorial Coordinator: Margaret Kelly

Photography: Quentin Bacon
Food and Styling: Donna Hay
Food Stylist's Assistant: Alexandra Tofield

DESIGN AND PRODUCTION
Managers: Sheridan Carter, Anna Maguire
Layout and Finished Art: Lulu Dougherty
Cover Design: Jenny Pace

Includes Index
ISBN 1 58279 340 9
EAN 9 781582 793405

First Edition Printed August 2001

Printed by Toppan Printed in China

THE PANTRY SHELF

Unless otherwise stated, the following ingredients used in this book are:

Cream	Double, suitable for whipping
Flour	White flour, plain or standard
Sugar	White sugar

WHAT'S IN A TABLESPOON?

AUSTRALIA
1 tablespoon = 20 mL OR 4 teaspoons

NEW ZEALAND
1 tablespoon = 15 mL OR 3 teaspoons

UNITED KINGDOM
1 tablespoon = 15 mL OR 3 teaspoons
The recipes in this book were tested in Australia where a 20 mL tablespoon is standard. All measures are level.

The tablespoon in the New Zealand and United Kingdom sets of measuring spoons is 15 mL. For recipes using baking powder, gelatine, bicarbonate of soda, small quantities of flour and cornflour, simply add another teaspoon for each tablespoon specified.

CANNED FOOD

Can sizes vary between countries and manufacturers. You may find the quantities in this book are slightly different from what is available. Purchase and use the can size nearest to the suggested size in the recipe.

MICROWAVE IT

Where microwave instructions occur in this book a microwave oven with a 650 watt output has been used. Wattage on domestic microwave ovens varies between 500 and 700 watts, so it may be necessary to vary cooking times slightly depending on the wattage of your oven.

CONTENTS

LIGHT AND FRESH

These healthy pasta dishes and delicious yet good-for-you pizzas will be adored by anyone looking for fresh ideas and interesting food. Pizzas and pasta are often associated with creamy sauces, masses of rich cheese and lots of olive oil. The recipes in this chapter keep these ingredients to a minimum while still retaining the traditional tastes of these ever-popular foods.

PENNE WITH SAFFRON AND PRAWNS

500 g/1 lb penne
500 g/1 lb cooked prawns, shelled
and deveined
125 g/4 oz snow peas (mangetout),
blanched

SAFFRON SAUCE
30 g/1 oz butter
1 tablespoon flour
1 cup/250 mL/8 fl oz reduced-fat milk
$^{1}/_{2}$ teaspoon saffron threads or pinch
saffron powder
1 tablespoon chopped fresh sage
or $^{1}/_{2}$ teaspoon dried sage

1 Cook pasta in boiling water in a large saucepan following packet directions. Drain, set aside and keep warm.

2 To make sauce, melt butter in a small saucepan over a medium heat, stir in flour and cook for 1 minute. Remove pan from heat and whisk in milk, saffron and sage. Return pan to heat and cook, stirring, for 3-4 minutes or until sauce boils and thickens.

3 Add prawns and snow peas (mangetout) to hot pasta and toss to combine. Top with sauce and serve immediately.

Serves 4

While saffron is an expensive spice you only require a little to add wonderful colour and flavour to food. Food flavoured with saffron has a distinctive aroma, a bitter honey-like taste and a strong yellow colour.

*Penne with Saffron and Prawns,
Pasta with Fresh Tomato Sauce (page 6)*

PASTA WITH FRESH TOMATO SAUCE

Parmesan cheese shavings make an elegant garnish for many pasta dishes. To make shavings, you will need a piece of fresh Parmesan cheese. Use a vegetable peeler or a coarse grater to remove shavings from cheese.
If rocket is unavailable use watercress instead.

500 g/1 lb angel's hair pasta
30 g/1 oz grated Parmesan cheese
185 g/6 oz rocket
fresh Parmesan cheese

FRESH TOMATO SAUCE
4 ripe large tomatoes, chopped
1/4 cup/60 mL/2 fl oz vegetable stock
1 tablespoon balsamic or
red wine vinegar
freshly ground black pepper

1   Cook pasta in boiling water in a large saucepan following packet directions. Drain, set aside and keep warm.

2   To make sauce, place tomatoes in a food processor or blender and process until smooth. With machine running, add stock, vinegar and black pepper to taste and process to combine.

3   Add grated Parmesan cheese to hot pasta and toss to combine. To serve, top pasta with sauce, rocket leaves and shavings of Parmesan cheese.

Serves 4

FETTUCCINE WITH SPINACH SAUCE

500 g/1 lb fettuccine
fresh Parmesan cheese

SPINACH SAUCE
15 g/1/2 oz butter
1 clove garlic, crushed
1 leek, sliced
1 bunch/500 g/1 lb English
spinach, chopped
250 g/8 oz reduced-fat cream cheese
2 tablespoons grated Parmesan cheese
1/2 cup/125 mL/4 fl oz chicken stock

1   Cook pasta in boiling water in a large saucepan, following packet directions. Drain, set aside and keep warm.

2   To make sauce, melt butter in a saucepan over a medium heat, add garlic and leek and cook, stirring, for 3 minutes. Add spinach and cook for 3 minutes longer or until spinach wilts.

3   Place spinach mixture, cream cheese, grated Parmesan cheese and stock in a food processor or blender and process until smooth. Return sauce to a clean saucepan, bring to simmering and simmer, stirring constantly, for 5-6 minutes or until sauce thickens and is heated through.

4   Spoon sauce over hot pasta and toss to combine. Serve topped with shavings of Parmesan cheese.

This pretty pasta dish is a perfect first course for a vegetarian meal. If serving as a starter this recipe will serve six.

Serves 4

LINGUINE WITH CHILLI AND LEMON

Linguine with Chilli and Lemon, Fettuccine with Spinach Sauce

500 g/1 lb fresh linguine or spaghetti
2 tablespoons olive oil
6 cloves garlic, peeled
2 fresh red chillies, seeded and sliced
125 g/4 oz rocket, shredded
3 teaspoons finely grated lemon rind
2 tablespoons lemon juice
freshly ground black pepper
90 g/3 oz grated Parmesan cheese

1   Cook pasta in boiling water in a large saucepan, following packet directions. Drain, set aside and keep warm.

2   Heat oil in a frying pan over a low heat, add garlic and chillies and cook, stirring, for 6 minutes or until garlic is golden. Add garlic mixture, rocket, lemon rind, lemon juice, black pepper to taste and Parmesan cheese to hot pasta and toss to combine.

Serves 4

Linguine is a long thin pasta with square-cut edges that comes from Campania in Southern Italy. If unavailable fettuccine, tagliatelle and spaghetti are all suitable alternatives.
If rocket is unavailable watercress can be used instead.

PESTO VEGETABLE CALZONE

Oven temperature
200°C, 400°F, Gas 6

Calzone is basically a pizza folded over to encase the filling. These individual calzone make great finger food for an informal party and leftovers are a welcome addition to a packed lunch.

2 quantities Basic Pizza
Dough (page 74)
olive oil

VEGETABLE AND
CHEESE FILLING
2 eggplant (aubergines), sliced
1 red pepper, chopped
1 green pepper, chopped
2 zucchini (courgettes), chopped
$^{3}/_{4}$ cup/185 g/6 oz ready-made pesto
4 bocconcini or 125 g/4 oz mozzarella
cheese, chopped
3 tablespoons pine nuts
freshly ground black pepper

1   To make filling, brush eggplant (aubergine) slices with a little oil and cook under a preheated hot grill for 3-4 minutes each side or until golden. Drain on absorbent kitchen paper and chop.

2   Heat 1 tablespoon oil in a frying pan over a medium heat, add red pepper, green pepper, zucchini (courgettes) and pesto and cook, stirring, for 3 minutes or until vegetables are soft. Mix in eggplant (aubergines) and set aside to cool.

3   Add cheese, pine nuts and black pepper to taste to vegetable mixture and mix to combine.

4   Prepare pizza dough as described in recipe. Divide dough into eight portions and shape each to form a 5 mm/$^{1}/_{4}$ in thick round with a 15 cm/6 in diameter. Place spoonfuls of filling in the centre of each dough round, brush the edges with water, then fold over to form a half circle. Press edges together to seal and using a fork make a decorative pattern.

5   Brush calzone with oil, place on lightly greased baking trays and bake for 20 minutes or until puffed and golden.

Makes 8

Pesto Vegetable Calzone

Sardine and Lime Pizza

SARDINE AND LIME PIZZA

1 quantity Basic Pizza Dough (page 74)

SARDINE AND ONION TOPPING
**2 teaspoons olive oil
3 red onions, sliced
3 cloves garlic, crushed
3 tablespoons chopped fresh
mixed herbs
2 x 100 g/3^1/$_2$ oz canned
sardines, drained
1 tablespoon finely grated lime rind
1 tablespoon lime juice
freshly ground black pepper**

Serves 4

1   Prepare pizza dough as described in recipe, then shape to form a 1 cm/^{1}/$_2$ in thick round with a 30 cm/12 in diameter. Place on a lightly greased baking tray and set aside.

2   To make topping, heat oil in a frying pan over a low heat. Add onions and garlic and cook, stirring, for 5 minutes or until onions are soft. Add herbs and mix to combine.

3   Spread onion mixture over pizza base, top with sardines, sprinkle with lime rind, lime juice and black pepper to taste. Bake for 10 minutes, then reduce oven temperature to 190°C/375°F/Gas 5 and bake for 15 minutes longer or until base is crisp and golden.

Oven temperature
220°C, 425°F, Gas 7

Use whatever herbs are in season for this pizza. For a traditional combination dill and parsley are delicious or for a Thai feel why not try coriander, basil and parsley.

GRILLED VEGETABLE PASTA

1 red pepper, seeded and
cut into quarters
1 yellow pepper, seeded and
cut into quarters
1 green pepper, seeded and
cut into quarters
6 baby eggplant (aubergines), cut
lengthwise into quarters
2 tablespoons olive oil
8 plum (egg or Italian) tomatoes, halved
8 slices prosciutto or lean ham
1 red onion, sliced
2 cloves garlic, crushed
1 tablespoon chopped fresh purple
basil or green basil
freshly ground black pepper
500 g/1 lb fresh spinach tagliatelle

1   Place red, yellow and green pepper quarters, skin side up, under a preheated hot grill and cook for 5-10 minutes until skins are blistered and charred. Place peppers in a plastic food bag and set aside until cool enough to handle. Remove skins from peppers and cut flesh into thick slices.

2   Brush cut surfaces of eggplant (aubergines) lightly with oil and cook under preheated hot grill for 2-3 minutes each side or until golden.

3   Place tomatoes, skin side down, under preheated hot grill and cook for 2 minutes or until soft.

4   Cook prosciutto or ham under preheated hot grill for 1 minute each side or until crisp. Drain on absorbent kitchen paper and set aside.

5   Heat remaining oil in a frying pan over a medium heat, add onion and garlic and cook, stirring, for 4 minutes or until onion is soft and golden. Add red pepper, yellow pepper, green pepper, eggplant (aubergines), tomatoes, basil and black pepper to taste and cook, stirring, for 4 minutes.

6   Cook pasta in boiling water in a large saucepan following packet directions. Drain well, top with vegetable mixture and prosciutto or ham slices. Serve immediately.

Serves 4

This pretty pasta dish is delightful for casual entertaining. A complete meal might start with a mixed green salad and crusty bread and finish with a selection of fresh seasonal fruit.
If plum (egg or Italian) tomatoes are unavailable use small ordinary tomatoes instead.

Grilled Vegetable Pasta

CHILLI PRAWN PIZZA

Oven temperature
200°C, 400°F, Gas 6

1 quantity Basic Pizza Dough (page 74)
3 tablespoons tomato paste (purée)
2 teaspoons vegetable oil
1 teaspoon ground cumin
3 fresh red chillies, seeded and chopped
2 cloves garlic, crushed
2 tablespoons lemon juice
500 g/1 lb uncooked prawns,
shelled and deveined
1 red pepper, sliced
1 yellow or green pepper, sliced
2 tablespoons chopped fresh coriander
2 tablespoons grated Parmesan cheese
freshly ground black pepper

For a complete meal
accompany this tasty pizza
with a salad of mixed
lettuces and fresh herbs.

1   Prepare pizza dough as described in recipe, then shape to form a 30 cm/12 in round. Place on a lightly greased baking tray, spread with tomato paste (purée) and set aside.

2   Heat oil in a frying pan over a medium heat, add cumin, chillies and garlic and cook, stirring, for 1 minute.

3   Stir in lemon juice and prawns and cook for 3 minutes longer or until prawns just change colour and are almost cooked.

4   Top pizza base with red pepper, yellow or green pepper, then with prawn mixture, coriander, Parmesan cheese and black pepper to taste. Bake for 20 minutes or until base is crisp and golden.

Serves 4

SALMON AND AVOCADO PIZZA

1 quantity Basic Pizza Dough (page 74)
200 g/6^1/$_2$ oz ricotta cheese, drained
2 tablespoons chopped fresh dill
1 tablespoon chopped fresh lemon
thyme or ^{1}/$_2$ teaspoon dried thyme and
1 teaspoon finely grated lemon rind
250 g/8 oz smoked salmon slices
1 avocado, stoned, peeled and sliced
1 tablespoon capers, drained
125 g/4 oz cherry tomatoes, halved

1   Prepare pizza dough as described in recipe, then press dough into a greased 26 x 32 cm/10^1/$_2$ x 12^3/$_4$ in Swiss roll tin. Set aside.

2   Place ricotta cheese, dill and thyme in a bowl and mix to combine. Spread ricotta mixture over pizza base and bake for 15 minutes.

3   Top pizza with smoked salmon, avocado slices, capers and tomatoes. Reduce oven temperature to 180°C/350°F/Gas 4 and bake for 10 minutes longer or until heated through and base is crisp and golden.

Left: Chilli Prawn Pizza
Above: Salmon and Avocado Pizza

Serves 4

Oven temperature
200°C, 400°F, Gas 6

In Italy the domestic pizza is often made with pastry rather than a yeast bread dough. You might like to try this alternative. Other easy bases include purchased focaccia bread, pitta bread rounds, hamburger buns and muffins. Different bases may affect the cooking time of your pizza.

YOGURT CHICKEN PIZZA

Oven temperature
200°C, 400°F, Gas 6

1 quantity Basic Pizza Dough (page 74)
$^1/_2$ cup/100 g/$3^1/_2$ oz low-fat
natural yogurt
1 tablespoon chopped fresh mint
1 tablespoon mango chutney
250 g/8 oz cooked chicken, chopped
1 red pepper, thinly sliced
1 tablespoon fresh coriander leaves
3 tablespoons pine nuts

1 Prepare pizza dough as described in recipe, then shape to form a 30 cm/12 in round. Place on a lightly greased baking tray and set aside.

2 Place yogurt, mint and chutney in a bowl and mix to combine. Spread yogurt mixture over pizza base and bake for 15 minutes.

3 Top pizza with chicken, red pepper, coriander leaves and pine nuts and bake for 10-15 minutes longer or until topping is heated through and base is crisp and golden.

Serves 4

A great way to turn leftover cooked chicken into something special. As a delicious alternative this pizza could be made with leftover cooked lamb.

PROSCIUTTO AND CHEESE CALZONE

Oven temperature
200°C, 400°F, Gas 6

2 quantities Basic Pizza
Dough (page 74)
olive oil

PROSCIUTTO AND
CHEESE FILLING
200 g/$6^1/_2$ oz ricotta cheese, drained
14 slices prosciutto or lean ham,
chopped
125 g/4 oz provolone or Parmesan
cheese, grated
30 g/1 oz sun-dried tomatoes, chopped
60 g/2 oz pitted black olives, chopped
2 tablespoons chopped fresh basil

1 To make filling, place ricotta cheese, prosciutto or ham, provolone or Parmesan cheese, sun-dried tomatoes, olives and basil in a bowl and mix to combine. Set aside.

2 Prepare pizza dough as described in recipe. Divide dough into eight portions and shape each to form a 5 mm/$^1/_4$ in thick round with a 15 cm/6 in diameter. Place spoonfuls of filling in the centre of each dough round, brush the edges with water, then fold over to form a half circle. Press edges together to seal and using a fork make a decorative pattern.

3 Brush calzone with oil, place on lightly greased baking trays and bake for 20 minutes or until puffed and golden.

Makes 8

A salad of mixed lettuces tossed with balsamic vinegar makes a wonderful accompaniment to these individual calzone.

Yogurt Chicken Pizza,
Prosciutto and Cheese Calzone

TOMATO AND CHEESE LASAGNE

Oven temperature
180°C, 350°F, Gas 4

If instant (no precooking required) lasagne is unavailable use dried lasagne instead, but cook it briefly before using. When using instant (no precooking required) lasagne the cooked dish tends to be moister and the pasta more tender if the lasagne sheets are dipped in warm water before assembling lasagne.

1 cup/250 g/8 oz ricotta cheese, drained
1 tablespoon chopped fresh parsley
1 tablespoon chopped fresh basil
freshly ground black pepper
60 g/2 oz grated pecorino or
Parmesan cheese
125 g/4 oz grated mozzarella cheese
9 sheets instant (no precooking
required) lasagne

FRESH TOMATO SAUCE
2 teaspoons olive oil
2 cloves garlic, crushed
1 onion, chopped
7 tomatoes, peeled, seeded and chopped
2 tablespoons tomato paste (purée)
1 bay leaf
3 sprigs fresh thyme or $^1/_2$ teaspoon
dried thyme
1 small ham or bacon bone
$^1/_2$ cup/125 mL/4 fl oz water
1 teaspoon sugar

1 Place ricotta cheese, parsley, basil and black pepper to taste in a bowl and mix to combine. Set aside.

2 Place pecorino or Parmesan and mozzarella cheeses in a bowl and mix to combine. Set aside.

3 To make sauce, heat oil in a saucepan over a medium heat, add garlic and onion and cook, stirring, for 3 minutes or until onion is soft. Add tomatoes and cook, stirring for 4 minutes longer.

4 Add tomato paste (purée), bay leaf, thyme, ham or bacon bone, water and sugar and bring to the boil. Reduce heat and simmer, stirring occasionally, for 45 minutes or until sauce reduces and thickens. Remove ham or bacon bone from sauce and discard.

5 Place three lasagne sheets in the base of a greased 18 x 28 cm/7 x 11 in ovenproof dish. Top with one-third of the tomato sauce, then one-third of the ricotta mixture and one-third of the cheese mixture. Repeat layers twice more to use all ingredients finishing with a layer of cheese. Bake for 30 minutes or until hot and bubbling and top is golden.

Serves 6

Tile and plate Lakeman Oldroyd

Left: Tomato and Cheese Lasagne
Right: Chicken and Mango Pasta Salad

Tile and plate Lakeman Oldroyd

CHICKEN AND MANGO PASTA SALAD

500 g/1 lb large shell pasta
1 cooked chicken, flesh cut into
bite-sized pieces
220 g/7 oz canned water chestnuts,
drained and sliced
440 g/14 oz canned mangoes,
drained and sliced

MANGO CHUTNEY DRESSING
1 cup/250 g/8 oz low-oil mayonnaise
¹/₂ cup/155 g/5 oz sweet mango chutney
2 spring onions, finely chopped
2 tablespoons chopped fresh coriander
freshly ground black pepper

1   Cook pasta in boiling water in a large
saucepan following packet directions.
Drain, rinse under cold running water and
drain again.

2   Place pasta, chicken, water chestnuts
and mangoes in a bowl and toss to
combine.

3   To make dressing, place mayonnaise,
chutney, spring onions, coriander and
black pepper to taste in a bowl and mix to
combine. Spoon dressing over salad and
toss to combine. Cover and chill until
required.

Serves 6

Pasta salads are a great
addition to a buffet or one
such as this is a substantial
one-dish meal. Leftover
cooked turkey is a tasty
alternative to chicken and
when fresh mangoes are in
season use these rather than
canned ones.

17

TAGLIATELLE WITH CHILLI OCTOPUS

1 kg/2 lb baby octopus, cleaned
500 g/1 lb spinach tagliatelle

CHILLI GINGER MARINADE
1 tablespoon sesame oil
1 tablespoon grated fresh ginger
2 tablespoons lime juice
2 tablespoon sweet chilli sauce

TOMATO SAUCE
2 teaspoons vegetable oil
3 spring onions, sliced diagonally
440 g/14 oz canned tomato
purée (passata)

As a main course all this dish needs is a sauté of mixed vegetables or a tossed green salad and crusty bread or rolls. It is delicious served on its own as a first course, in which case it will serve six. This is also delicious made with calamari (squid) rings instead of octopus.

1   To make marinade, place sesame oil, ginger, lime juice and chilli sauce in a large bowl and mix to combine. Add octopus, toss to coat, cover and marinate in the refrigerator for 3-4 hours.

2   Cook pasta in boiling water in a large saucepan following packet directions. Drain, set aside and keep warm.

3   To make sauce, heat oil in a saucepan over a medium heat. Add spring onions and cook, stirring, for 1 minute. Stir in tomato purée (passata), bring to simmering and simmer for 4 minutes.

4   Cook octopus under a preheated hot grill for 5-7 minutes or until tender. Add octopus to sauce and toss to combine. Spoon octopus mixture over hot pasta and toss to combine.

Serves 4

PASTA WITH AVOCADO SAUCE

500 g/1 lb pasta shapes of your choice
125 g/4 oz snow peas
(mangetout), trimmed
125 g/4 oz yellow squash or
zucchini (courgettes), sliced
fresh Parmesan cheese (optional)

AVOCADO SAUCE
1 avocado, stoned and peeled
1 cup/250 g/8 oz ricotta cheese, drained
1 tablespoon lime juice
2 teaspoons finely grated lime rind
2 tablespoons milk
2 tablespoons chopped fresh coriander
freshly ground black pepper

To make shavings of
Parmesan cheese see hint
on page 6.

1   Cook pasta in boiling water in a large saucepan following packet directions. Drain, set aside and keep warm.

2   To make sauce, place avocado, ricotta cheese, lime juice, lime rind, milk, coriander and black pepper to taste in a food processor or blender and process until smooth. Set aside.

3   Boil, steam or microwave snow peas (mangetout) and squash or zucchini (courgettes) separately until just tender. Drain well. Add vegetables to hot pasta and toss to combine. To serve, top pasta with sauce and shavings of Parmesan cheese, if using.

Serves 6

*Pasta with Avocado Sauce,
Tagliatelle with Chilli Octopus*

THE CLASSICS

*In this chapter you will find those often forgotten old favourites.
There are recipes for Spaghetti Bolognaise, Spaghetti Marinara,
Pizza Supremo and the all-time favourite Macaroni Cheese.
This is the chapter you will turn to time and again when you are
looking for that traditional recipe like Mama used to make.*

PIZZA SUPREMO

Oven temperature
200°C, 400°F, Gas 6

2 quantities Basic Pizza
Dough (page 74)
³/4 cup/185 mL/6 fl oz tomato
paste (purée)
1 green pepper, chopped
155 g/5 oz sliced peperoni or salami
155 g/5 oz ham or prosciutto, sliced
125 g/4 oz mushrooms, sliced
440 g/14 oz canned pineapple
pieces, drained
60 g/2 oz pitted olives
125 g/4 oz mozzarella cheese, grated
125 g/4 oz tasty cheese (mature
Cheddar), grated

1   Prepare pizza dough as described in
recipe. Divide dough into two portions
and shape each to form a 30 cm/12 in
round. Place rounds on lightly greased
baking trays and spread with tomato
paste (purée).

2   Arrange half the green pepper,
peperoni or salami, ham or prosciutto,
mushrooms, pineapple and olives
attractively on each pizza base.

3   Combine mozzarella cheese and tasty
cheese (mature Cheddar) and sprinkle
half the mixture over each pizza. Bake for
25-30 minutes or until cheese is golden
and base is crisp.

Serves 8

If you only want to make one
pizza, halve the topping
ingredients and use only one
quantity of dough. But
remember everyone loves
pizza and they always eat
more than you – or they –
think they will.

Pizza Supremo

FETTUCCINE CARBONARA

500 g/1 lb fettuccine

CARBONARA SAUCE
250 g/8 oz ham, prosciutto or bacon, chopped
1/2 cup/125 mL/4 fl oz chicken stock
1 cup/250 mL/8 fl oz cream (double)
7 eggs, lightly beaten
2 tablespoons chopped flat-leaf parsley
freshly ground black pepper

This dish is very rich and needs only to be accompanied by a green salad and some crusty bread. It makes a great special occasion treat, but care should be taken not to overcook sauce. Once the pasta is added to the sauce its heat will also help to cook it. This dish can use any ribbon pasta.

1 Cook pasta in boiling water in a large saucepan following packet directions. Drain, set aside and keep warm.

2 To make sauce, cook ham, prosciutto or bacon in a frying pan over a medium heat for 3 minutes or until crisp.

3 Stir in stock and cream, bring to simmering and simmer until sauce is reduced by half.

4 Remove pan from heat, whisk in eggs, parsley and black pepper to taste. Return pan to heat and cook, stirring, for 1 minute. Remove pan from heat, add hot pasta to sauce and toss to combine. Serve immediately.

Serves 6

Tile Lakeman Oldroyd

PENNE NAPOLITANA

500 g/1 lb penne
fresh Parmesan cheese

NAPOLITANA SAUCE
2 teaspoons olive oil
2 onions, chopped
2 cloves garlic, crushed
2 x 440 g/14 oz canned tomatoes,
undrained and mashed
$^3/_4$ cup/185 mL/6 fl oz red wine
1 tablespoon chopped flat-leaf parsley
1 tablespoon chopped fresh oregano or
$^1/_2$ teaspoon dried oregano
freshly ground black pepper

1 Cook pasta in boiling water in a large saucepan following packet directions. Drain, set aside and keep warm.

2 To make sauce, heat oil in a saucepan over a medium heat. Add onions and garlic and cook, stirring, for 3 minutes or until onions are soft.

3 Stir in tomatoes, wine, parsley, oregano and black pepper to taste, bring to simmering and simmer for 15 minutes or until sauce reduces and thickens.

4 To serve, spoon sauce over hot pasta and top with shavings of Parmesan cheese.

Serves 4

Left: Fettuccine Carbonara
Above: Penne Napolitana

To make shavings of Parmesan cheese see hint on page 6.
Penne is a short tubular pasta similar to macaroni, but with the ends cut at an angle rather than straight. If penne is unavailable macaroni is a suitable alternative for this recipe.

THREE-CHEESE PIZZA

Oven temperature
200°C, 400°F, Gas 6

1 quantity Basic Pizza Dough (page 74)
2 teaspoons vegetable oil

CHEESE TOPPING
200 g/6^1/$_2$ oz blue cheese, crumbled
60 g/2 oz pine nuts
125 g/4 oz mozzarella cheese, grated
2 tablespoons fresh oregano leaves or
^{1}/$_2$ teaspoon dried oregano
90 g/3 oz grated Parmesan cheese
freshly ground black pepper

1   Prepare pizza dough as described in recipe. Remove about one-quarter of the dough and set aside. Press remaining dough into a lightly greased 26 x 32 cm/ 10^1/$_2$ x 12^3/$_4$ in Swiss roll tin and brush with oil.

2   Roll reserved dough into two sausage shapes each 26 cm/10^1/$_2$ in long. Place these across the pizza base to divide it into three equal portions.

3   Top one-third of the pizza with the blue cheese and pine nuts. Another third with the mozzarella cheese and oregano leaves and the remaining third with the Parmesan cheese and black pepper to taste. Bake for 20-25 minutes or until cheese is golden and base is crisp.

Serves 4

Serve this deliciously rich cheese pizza with a salad of raw or steamed mixed vegetables tossed in a light French or Italian dressing.

ORIGINAL TOMATO PIZZAS

Oven temperature
200°C, 400°F, Gas 6

2 quantities Basic Pizza
Dough (page 74)
olive oil
5 ripe tomatoes, sliced
4 cloves garlic, sliced
4 tablespoons fresh oregano leaves
freshly ground black pepper

1   Prepare pizza dough as described in recipe. Divide dough into two portions and shape each to form a 30 cm/12 in round. Place rounds on lightly greased baking trays and brush with oil.

2   Arrange half the tomato slices, garlic and oregano on top of each pizza base and season to taste with black pepper. Bake for 15-20 minutes or until base is crisp and golden.

Serves 8

The simplest pizza of all, this one is best made with fresh young garlic. Any fresh herbs can be used in place of the oregano – marjoram, thyme and basil are all delicious alternatives.

Three-Cheese Pizza, Original Tomato Pizza

FRENCH PISSALADIERE

Oven temperature
200°C, 400°F, Gas 6

2 quantities Basic Pizza
Dough (page 74)
24 anchovy fillets
125 g/4 oz pitted black olives
2 tablespoons capers, drained
60 g/2 oz pine nuts
freshly ground black pepper

ONION TOPPING
2 tablespoons olive oil
8 onions, thinly sliced
6 cloves garlic, crushed
2 tablespoons chopped fresh thyme or
1 teaspoon dried thyme
2 tablespoons sugar

Originating from the
Provence region of France
this delicious onion, anchovy
and olive topped bread is
the French equivalent of the
Italian pizza.

Serves 8

1   Prepare pizza dough as described in recipe. Divide dough into two portions and press each into a lightly greased 26 x 32 cm/10^1/2 x 12^3/4 in Swiss roll tin.

2   To make topping, heat oil in a large saucepan over a medium heat. Add onions and garlic and cook, stirring, for 10 minutes or until onions are soft. Reduce heat to low, add thyme and sugar and cook, stirring frequently, for 20 minutes or until mixture is thick and caramelised.

3   Spread half the onion mixture over each pizza base, then top with anchovy fillets, olives, capers, pine nuts and black pepper to taste. Bake for 20-25 minutes or until base is crisp and golden.

FETTUCCINE PESTO

500 g/1 lb fettuccine

BASIL PESTO
100 g/3$^1/_2$ oz fresh Parmesan cheese,
chopped
2 cloves garlic, crushed
60 g/2 oz pine nuts
1 large bunch basil, leaves removed and
stems discarded
$^1/_4$ cup/60 mL/2 fl oz olive oil

Left: French Pissaladière
Below: Fettuccine Pesto

1   Cook pasta in boiling water in a large saucepan following packet directions. Drain, set aside and keep warm.

2   To make pesto, place Parmesan cheese, garlic, pine nuts and basil in a food processor or blender and process to finely chop. With machine running, gradually add oil and continue processing to form a smooth paste. To serve, spoon pesto over hot pasta and toss to combine.

Serves 4

Basil is one of the herbs that characterises Italian cooking. This pesto can be made when basil is plentiful, then frozen and used as required. Treat yourself to this dish in mid-winter to remind you of balmy summer days.

Tile Lakeman Oldroyd Bowls Pillivuyt

SPAGHETTI BOLOGNAISE

500 g/1 lb spaghetti
grated Parmesan cheese (optional)

BOLOGNAISE SAUCE
2 teaspoons vegetable oil
1 clove garlic, crushed
1 onion, chopped
500 g/1 lb beef mince
440 g/14 oz canned tomato purée
(passata)
$^1/_4$ cup/60 mL/2 fl oz red wine or water
1 tablespoon chopped fresh oregano or
$^1/_2$ teaspoon dried oregano
1 tablespoon chopped fresh thyme or
$^1/_2$ teaspoon dried thyme
freshly ground black pepper

For an easy family meal serve this all-time favourite with steamed vegetables or a tossed green salad and crusty bread or rolls.

1   To make sauce, heat oil in a frying pan over a medium heat. Add garlic and onion and cook, stirring, for 3 minutes or until onion is soft.

2   Add beef and cook, stirring, for 5 minutes or until meat is well browned. Stir in tomato purée (passata), wine or water, oregano and thyme. Bring to simmering and simmer, stirring occasionally, for 15 minutes or until sauce reduces and thickens. Season to taste with black pepper.

3   Cook pasta in boiling water in a large saucepan following packet directions. Drain well. To serve, spoon sauce over hot pasta and top with Parmesan cheese, if using.

Serves 4

GNOCCHI WITH GORGONZOLA SAUCE

500 g/1 lb potato gnocchi

GORGONZOLA SAUCE
200 g/6$^1/_2$ oz Gorgonzola or blue cheese,
crumbled
$^3/_4$ cup/185 mL/6 fl oz milk
60 g/2 oz butter
60 g/2 oz walnuts, toasted and chopped
200 mL /6$^1/_2$ fl oz cream (double)
freshly ground black pepper

Potato gnocchi is available from speciality pasta shops. This sauce is also great with shell pasta, penne, macaroni, tortellini or farfalle.

1   Cook gnocchi in boiling water in a large saucepan following packet directions. Drain, set aside and keep warm.

2   To make sauce, place Gorgonzola or blue cheese, milk and butter in a saucepan and cook over a low heat, stirring, for 4-5 minutes or until cheese melts. Stir in walnuts, cream and black pepper to taste, bring to simmering and simmer for 5 minutes or until sauce reduces and thickens. Spoon sauce over hot gnocchi and toss to combine.

Serves 6

*Gnocchi with Gorgonzola Sauce,
Spaghetti Bolognaise*

SPAGHETTI MARINARA

500 g/1 lb spaghetti
2 teaspoons vegetable oil
2 teaspoons butter
2 onions, chopped
2 x 440 g/14 oz canned tomatoes,
undrained and mashed
2 tablespoons chopped fresh basil or
1 teaspoon dried basil
^{1}/4 cup/60 mL/2 fl oz dry white wine
12 mussels, scrubbed and beards
removed
12 scallops
12 uncooked prawns, shelled and
deveined
125 g/4 oz calamari (squid) rings

1   Cook pasta in boiling water in a large
saucepan following packet directions.
Drain, set aside and keep warm.

2   Heat oil and butter in a frying pan
over a medium heat. Add onions and
cook, stirring, for 4 minutes or until
onions are golden.

3   Stir in tomatoes, basil and wine, bring
to simmering and simmer for 8 minutes.
Add mussels, scallops and prawns and
cook for 2 minutes longer.

4   Add calamari (squid) and cook for 1
minute or until shellfish is cooked. Spoon
shellfish mixture over hot pasta and serve
immediately.

Serves 4

Another traditional favourite
that can be made using
whatever seafood is
available. The tomato base
for the sauce can be made
in advance and frozen if you
wish. While the pasta is
cooking, reheat the sauce
and add the seafood as
directed in the recipe.

TORTELLINI BOSCAIOLA

750 g/1^1/2 lb tortellini
grated Parmesan cheese (optional)

CREAMY MUSHROOM SAUCE
15 g/^{1}/2 oz butter
4 spring onions, chopped
250 g/8 oz ham, thinly sliced
250 g/8 oz mushrooms, sliced
1 cup/250 mL/8 fl oz chicken stock
2 cups/500 mL/16 fl oz cream (double)
freshly ground black pepper

1   Cook pasta in boiling water in a large
saucepan following packet directions.
Drain, set aside and keep warm.

2   To make sauce, melt butter in a frying
pan over a medium heat. Add spring
onions, ham and mushrooms and cook,
stirring, for 4 minutes or until mushrooms
are soft.

3   Stir in stock, cream and black pepper
to taste, bring to simmering and simmer
for 6-8 minutes or until sauce reduces and
thickens slightly.

4   To serve, spoon sauce over hot pasta,
toss to combine and top with Parmesan
cheese, if using.

Serves 6

If the word *boscaiola*
appears in the name of an
Italian dish it indicates that it
contains mushrooms in some
form or other. You might like
to try this creamy mushroom
sauce with other pastas such
as tagliatelle, fettuccine or
penne.

FETTUCCINE ALFREDO

Fettuccine Alfredo, Spaghetti Marinara, Tortellini Boscaiola

500 g/1 lb fettuccine
155 g/5 oz butter, softened and chopped
125 g/4 oz grated fresh Parmesan cheese
freshly ground black pepper

1   Cook pasta in boiling water in a large saucepan following packet directions. Drain well and place in a large serving bowl.

2   Scatter butter and Parmesan cheese over hot pasta, season to taste with black pepper, toss and serve immediately.

Serves 4

So simple, yet so delicious. For a complete meal, serve with a tossed green salad and crusty bread and finish with a selection of fresh seasonal fruit.

TRADITIONAL LASAGNE

24 sheets instant (no precooking required) lasagne
60 g/2 oz mozzarella cheese, grated

CHEESE SAUCE
75 g/2¹/₂ oz butter
¹/₃ cup/45 g/1¹/₂ oz flour
2 cups/500 mL/16 fl oz milk
90 g/3 oz tasty cheese (mature Cheddar), grated
freshly ground black pepper

MEAT SAUCE
2 teaspoons vegetable oil
2 onions, chopped
2 cloves garlic, crushed
1.25 kg/2¹/₂ lb beef mince
2 x 440 g/14 oz canned tomatoes, undrained and mashed
³/₄ cup/185 mL/6 fl oz red wine
2 tablespoons chopped mixed herbs

Oven temperature
180°C, 350°F, Gas 4

Lasagne is delicious served with a salad of lightly cooked mixed vegetables tossed with an Italian dressing.

1 To make Cheese Sauce, melt butter in a saucepan over a medium heat. Stir in flour and cook, stirring, for 1 minute. Remove pan from heat and whisk in milk. Return pan to heat and cook, stirring, for 4-5 minutes or until sauce boils and thickens. Stir in cheese and black pepper to taste and set aside.

2 To make Meat Sauce, heat oil in a frying pan over a medium heat. Add onions and garlic and cook, stirring, for 3 minutes or until onions are soft. Add beef and cook, stirring, for 5 minutes or until beef is brown. Stir in tomatoes, wine and herbs, bring to simmering and simmer, stirring occasionally, for 15 minutes or until sauce reduces and thickens. Season to taste with black pepper.

3 Line the base of a large greased baking dish with 6 lasagne sheets. Top with one-quarter of the Meat Sauce and one-quarter of the Cheese Sauce. Repeat layers to use all ingredients, ending with a layer of Cheese Sauce.

4 Sprinkle top of lasagne with mozzarella cheese and bake for 30-40 minutes or until hot and bubbling and top is golden.

Serves 6

Tile Lakeman Oldroyd *Blue plate* Country Road *White plate* Pillivuyt

Left: Traditional Lasagne
Right: Macaroni Cheese

The Lakeman Oldroyd *Plate Country Road*

MACARONI CHEESE

315 g/10 oz macaroni
125 g/4 oz tasty cheese (mature
Cheddar), grated

CHEESE SAUCE
75 g/2^1/$_2$ oz butter
^{1}/$_3$ cup/45 g/1^1/$_2$ oz flour
1 teaspoon dry mustard
2^1/$_2$ cups/600 mL/1 pt milk
90 g/3 oz tasty cheese (mature
Cheddar), grated
freshly black ground pepper

Serves 6

1   Cook pasta in boiling water in a large saucepan following packet directions. Drain well and turn into a greased large ovenproof dish.

2   To make sauce, melt butter in a saucepan over a medium heat. Stir in flour and mustard and cook, stirring, for 1 minute. Remove pan from heat and whisk in milk. Return pan to heat and cook, stirring, for 5-6 minutes or until sauce boils and thickens. Stir in cheese and black pepper to taste.

3   Pour sauce over pasta, sprinkle with cheese and bake for 20-25 minutes or until hot and bubbling and top is golden.

Oven temperature
180°C, 350°F, Gas 4

You can vary this popular family favourite by adding chopped ham, chopped red or green peppers, finely chopped onion or chopped fresh parsley to the sauce.

JUST VEGETABLES

Top a pizza with an interesting combination of vegetables or toss pasta with lightly cooked vegetables and you have a wonderful dish that requires little else to make a complete meal. Vegetarians will love the recipes in this chapter, while others will be inspired to serve a meatless meal every once in a while.

BAKED VEGETABLE PAPPARDELLE

Oven temperature
220°C, 425°F, Gas 7

3 large eggplant (aubergines),
thinly sliced
salt
3 tablespoons olive oil
1 onion, chopped
2 cloves garlic, crushed
2 x 440 g/14 oz canned tomatoes,
undrained and mashed
$^1/_2$ teaspoon sugar
freshly ground black pepper
375 g/12 oz pappardelle
300 g/9$^1/_2$ oz mascarpone or
ricotta cheese
200 g/6$^1/_2$ oz grated mozzarella cheese

1   Sprinkle eggplant (aubergine) slices with salt, place in a colander and drain for 10 minutes. Rinse under cold running water and pat dry.

2   Place all but 2 teaspoons of oil in a frying pan and heat over a medium heat. Cook eggplant (aubergine) slices a few at a time for 3-4 minutes each side or until golden. Drain on absorbent kitchen paper.

3   Heat remaining oil in frying pan, add onion and garlic and cook, stirring, for 3 minutes or until onion is soft. Stir in tomatoes, sugar and black pepper to taste, bring to simmering and simmer, stirring occasionally, for 15 minutes or until mixture reduces and thickens.

4   Cook pasta in boiling water in a large saucepan for 10 minutes or until almost cooked. Drain well. Add tomato mixture to pasta and toss to combine.

5   Spread half the pasta mixture over the base of a lightly greased 2 litre/3$^1/_2$ pt capacity ovenproof dish. Top with half the eggplant (aubergine) slices, half the mascarpone or ricotta cheese and half the mozzarella cheese. Repeat layers finishing with a layer of mozzarella cheese and bake for 20 minutes or until hot and bubbling.

Serves 6

Pappardelle is a very wide ribbon pasta that was traditionally served with a sauce made of hare, herbs and wine, but today it is teamed with any rich sauce. If it is unavailable fettuccine can be used instead.

*Baked Vegetable Pappardelle,
Farfalle with Spring Vegetables (page 36)*

FARFALLE WITH SPRING VEGETABLES

500 g/1 lb farfalle
15 g/¹/₂ oz butter
2 spring onions, finely chopped
1 teaspoon finely grated orange rind
1¹/₂ cups/375 mL/12 fl oz cream (double)
1 cup/250 mL/8 fl oz vegetable stock
250 g/8 oz broccoli, cut into florets
250 g/8 oz asparagus spears, cut into 4 cm/1¹/₂ in lengths
125 g/4 oz snow peas (mangetout)
1 tablespoon finely chopped fresh mint
30 g/1 oz pine nuts, toasted

1   Cook pasta in boiling water in a large saucepan following packet directions. Drain, set aside and keep warm.

2   Melt butter in a frying pan over a medium heat. Add spring onions and cook, stirring, for 2 minutes. Stir in orange rind, cream and stock, bring to simmering and simmer for 10 minutes.

3   Add broccoli, asparagus, snow peas (mangetout) and mint to cream mixture and cook, stirring occasionally, for 5 minutes or until vegetables are tender. To serve, spoon vegetable mixture over hot pasta, toss to combine and sprinkle with pine nuts.

Serves 4

Farfalle means butterflies and this is what this pretty bow-shaped pasta looks like.

PASTA WITH SIX HERB SAUCE

500 g/1 lb pasta shapes of your choice

SIX HERB SAUCE
30 g/1 oz butter
2 tablespoons chopped fresh rosemary
12 small fresh sage leaves
12 small fresh basil leaves
2 tablespoons fresh marjoram leaves
2 tablespoons fresh oregano leaves
2 tablespoons chopped fresh parsley
2 cloves garlic, chopped
¹/₄ cup/60 mL/2 fl oz white wine
¹/₄ cup/60 mL/2 fl oz vegetable stock

1   Cook pasta in boiling water in a large saucepan following packet directions. Drain, set aside and keep warm.

2   To make sauce, melt butter in a saucepan over a medium heat. Add rosemary, sage, basil, marjoram, oregano, parsley and garlic and cook, stirring, for 1 minute.

3   Stir in wine and stock, bring to simmering and simmer for 4 minutes. To serve, spoon sauce over hot pasta and toss to combine.

Serves 4

Equally delicious as a light meal or the first course of a dinner party this dish must be made using fresh not dried herbs. However the herbs can be changed according to what is available. If you can only get four of the herbs then just use those.

Pasta with Six Herb Sauce

EASY CHILLI BEAN PIZZA

Oven temperature
220°C, 425°F, Gas 7

For those who are not fond of
chilli ordinary baked beans
can be used for this pizza
instead. If you wish to make
your own pizza base see the
recipe for Basic Pizza Dough
on page 74.

1 x 25 cm/10 in pizza base, homemade
or purchased
440 g/14 oz canned Mexican chilli beans
2 jalapeño chillies, seeded and sliced
250 g/8 oz grated mozzarella cheese
freshly ground black pepper
30 g/1 oz packet corn chips
3 tablespoons sour cream

1   Place pizza base on a lightly greased
baking tray and top with beans. Sprinkle
with chillies, mozzarella cheese and black
pepper to taste.

2   Bake for 15-20 minutes or until base is
crisp and golden. To serve, top pizza with
corn chips and sour cream.

Serves 4

Board Appley Hoare

GARDEN PIZZA

Left: Easy Chilli Bean Pizza
Above: Garden Pizza

1 quantity Basic Pizza Dough (page 74)

GARDEN TOPPING
250 g/8 oz asparagus spears, cut into
4 cm/1½ in pieces
125 g/4 oz baby yellow squash or
zucchini (courgettes), sliced
3 spring onions, chopped
155 g/5 oz broccoli, cut into florets
125 g/4 oz small peas
2 tablespoons chopped fresh basil or
1 teaspoon dried basil
60 g/2 oz grated mozzarella cheese
60 g/2 oz grated Parmesan cheese
freshly ground black pepper

1   Prepare pizza dough as described in recipe, then shape into a 30 cm/12 in round and place on a lightly greased baking tray.

2   Arrange asparagus, squash or zucchini (courgettes), spring onions, broccoli, peas and basil over dough. Sprinkle with mozzarella cheese, Parmesan cheese and black pepper to taste and bake for 20-25 minutes or until cheese is golden and base is crisp.

Serves 4

Oven temperature
200°C, 400°F, Gas 6

Remember that pizzas do not have to be large and round. Some are rectangles, some oval, some small individual circles and some have a deep crust and sides more resembling a pie (which after all, is what pizza means in Italian). So make your pizzas whatever shape you like.

39

PESTO PIZZETTE

Oven temperature
180°C, 350°F, Gas 4

These individual pizzas are a hit as finger food with young and old alike. Just as delicious cold, as they are hot, any leftovers will be a welcome addition to a packed lunch.
Roasted red peppers, chopped can be used in place of sun-dried peppers if you wish.

1 quantity Basic Pizza Dough (page 74)
200 g/6^1/$_2$ oz ricotta cheese
^{1}/$_2$ cup/125 g/4 oz ready-made pesto
2 teaspoons olive oil
2 leeks, sliced
125 g/4 oz button mushrooms, sliced
1 tablespoon brown sugar
100 g/3^1/$_2$ oz sun-dried peppers, chopped
250 g/8 oz yellow teardrop or cherry tomatoes, halved
1 tablespoon chopped fresh basil or 1 teaspoon dried basil
125 g/4 oz mozzarella cheese, grated

1   Prepare pizza dough as described in recipe. Divide dough into four portions and shape each to form a 15 cm/6 in round. Place rounds on lightly greased baking trays and set aside.

2   Place ricotta cheese and pesto in a bowl and mix to combine. Spread pesto mixture over dough and bake for 10 minutes.

3   Heat oil in a frying pan over a medium heat. Add leeks, mushrooms and sugar and cook, stirring, for 4 minutes or until vegetables are soft. Spread leek mixture over pesto mixture and top with sun-dried peppers, tomatoes and basil, sprinkle with cheese and bake for 20-25 minutes or until bases are crisp.

Makes 4

HERBED RICOTTA PIZZA

Oven temperature
220°C, 425°F, Gas 7

If different coloured zucchini (courgettes) are unavailable just use one colour – the pizza will still look impressive and tastes just the same.

1 quantity Basic Pizza Dough (page 74)
200 g/6^1/$_2$ oz ricotta cheese
2 tablespoons chopped fresh basil
2 tablespoons chopped fresh thyme
2 tablespoons chopped fresh oregano
2 green zucchini (courgettes), sliced
2 yellow zucchini (courgettes), sliced
freshly ground black pepper
60 g/2 oz grated Parmesan cheese

1   Prepare pizza dough as described in recipe then shape into a 30 cm/12 in round and place on a lightly greased baking tray.

2   Place ricotta cheese, basil, thyme and oregano in a food processor and process until smooth, then spread over dough. Starting in the centre of the pizza, arrange alternate coloured zucchini (courgette) slices in a spiral pattern on top of ricotta mixture. Season to taste with black pepper, sprinkle with Parmesan cheese and bake for 20 minutes or until base is crisp and golden.

Serves 4

Herbed Ricotta Pizza, Pesto Pizzette

Above: Hearty Macaroni Soup
Right: Spiral Pasta Salad

HEARTY MACARONI SOUP

This hearty pasta and vegetable soup makes a substantial one-dish meal. While the recipe uses macaroni you can in fact use any pasta you wish. Soups are a great way of using up any odds and ends of pasta you may have in the cupboard.

2 teaspoons vegetable oil
1 red onion, chopped
2 fresh red chillies, seeded and finely chopped
1 red pepper, chopped
2 carrots, chopped
2 zucchini (courgettes), sliced
4 cups/1 litre/1¾ pts vegetable stock
440 g/14 oz canned tomatoes, undrained and mashed
250 g/8 oz elbow macaroni
440 g/14 oz canned red kidney beans, rinsed
1 tablespoon finely chopped fresh thyme or ½ teaspoon dried thyme
200 g/6½ oz firm tofu, chopped
freshly ground black pepper

1   Heat oil in a large saucepan over a medium heat. Add onion and chillies and cook, stirring, for 3 minutes or until onion is soft.

2   Add red pepper, carrots, zucchini (courgettes), stock, tomatoes and macaroni, bring to simmering and simmer for 10 minutes or until macaroni is cooked.

3   Stir in beans, thyme and tofu, bring to simmering and simmer for 2 minutes or until heated through. Season to taste with black pepper.

Serves 4

Spiral Pasta Salad

500 g/1 lb spiral pasta
100 g/3½ oz sun-dried tomatoes, thinly
sliced
100 g/3½ oz marinated artichoke
hearts, chopped
75 g/2½ oz sun-dried or roasted
peppers, chopped
125 g/4 oz marinated black olives
12 small fresh basil leaves
60 g/2 oz Parmesan cheese shavings
1 tablespoon olive oil
3 tablespoons balsamic or red wine
vinegar

1   Cook pasta in boiling water in a large
saucepan following packet directions.
Drain, rinse under cold running water and
set aside to cool completely.

2   Place pasta, sun-dried tomatoes,
artichokes, sun-dried or roasted peppers,
olives, basil, Parmesan cheese, oil and
vinegar in a bowl and toss to combine.
Cover and refrigerate for 2 hours or until
ready to serve.

Serves 4

A wonderful salad that combines all the best flavours of Italy. It is delicious served with crusty bread and baked ricotta cheese. If you can, make it a day in advance so that the flavours have time to develop. To make shavings of Parmesan cheese see hint on page 6.

Tile and plate Lakeman Oldroyd

FOREST MUSHROOM PASTA

375 g/12 oz pasta of your choice
2 teaspoons vegetable oil
1 clove garlic, crushed
750 g/1¹/₂ lb mixed mushrooms

WHITE SAUCE
30 g/1 oz butter
2 tablespoons flour
2 cups/500 mL/16 fl oz milk
¹/₂ teaspoon ground nutmeg
freshly ground black pepper

1   Cook pasta in boiling water in a large saucepan following packet directions. Drain, set aside and keep warm.

2   To make sauce, melt butter in a saucepan over a medium heat. Stir in flour and cook, stirring, for 1 minute. Remove pan from heat and whisk in milk. Return pan to heat and cook, stirring, until sauce boils and thickens. Stir in nutmeg and season to taste with black pepper. Add sauce to pasta and mix to combine. Set aside and keep warm.

3   Heat oil in a frying pan over a medium heat. Add garlic and mushrooms and cook, stirring, for 4 minutes or until mushrooms are soft. To serve, top pasta with mushroom mixture.

Serves 4

If you can only get ordinary mushrooms add a few dried mushrooms for extra flavour. You will need to soak the dried mushrooms in boiling water for 20 minutes or until they are soft. Drain well, then slice or chop and add to the fresh mushrooms when cooking. Dried mushrooms have a strong flavour and you only need a few to add flavour.

RAVIOLI WITH WALNUT SAUCE

750 g/1¹/₂ lb cheese and spinach ravioli

WALNUT SAUCE
200 g/6¹/₂ oz walnuts
¹/₂ bunch fresh basil, leaves removed
and stems discarded
45 g/1¹/₂ oz butter, softened
45 g/1¹/₂ oz grated Parmesan cheese
freshly ground black pepper
100 mL/3¹/₂ fl oz olive oil
155 mL/5 fl oz cream (double)

1   Cook ravioli in boiling water in a large saucepan following packet directions. Drain, set aside and keep warm.

2   To make sauce, place walnuts and basil in a food processor or blender and process until finely chopped. Add butter, Parmesan cheese and black pepper to taste. With machine running, slowly add oil and cream and process until it is just combined. To serve, spoon sauce over pasta and toss.

Serves 4

Take care when making the sauce only process it briefly or until the ingredients are just combined once the cream is added. If you overprocess the cream may separate and cause the sauce to curdle.

*Ravioli with Walnut Sauce,
Forest Mushroom Pasta*

VEGETABLE CANNELLONI

Oven temperature
180°C, 350°F, Gas 4

Fresh or packaged dried pasta? Which is the best? Neither is superior – they are just different. Fresh pasta is more delicate and keeps for only a few days, while dried pasta is more robust and ideal for serving with heartier sauces.

12 instant (no precooking required)
cannelloni tubes
250 g/8 oz mozzarella cheese, grated

LEEK AND SPINACH FILLING
2 teaspoons olive oil
1 clove garlic, crushed
2 spring onions, finely chopped
2 leeks, thinly sliced
1 red pepper, sliced
1 bunch/500 g/1 lb English spinach,
chopped
200 g/6$^1/_2$ oz ricotta cheese, drained
315 g/10 oz canned creamed
sweet corn
2 teaspoons ground paprika

TOMATO SAUCE
1 teaspoon olive oil
1 onion, chopped
440 g/14 oz canned tomato purée
2 tablespoons dry white wine

1   To make filling, heat oil in a frying pan over a medium heat. Add garlic, spring onions and leeks and cook, stirring, for 4 minutes or until leeks are soft.

2   Add red pepper and spinach and cook, stirring, for 3 minutes or until spinach wilts. Drain off liquid.

3   Transfer vegetable mixture to a large bowl, add ricotta cheese, sweet corn and paprika and mix well to combine.

4   Spoon filling into cannelloni tubes and place tubes side-by-side in a greased large ovenproof dish. Set aside.

5   To make sauce, heat oil in a saucepan over a medium heat. Add onion and cook, stirring, for 3 minutes or until onion is soft. Stir in tomato purée and wine, bring to simmering and simmer for 4 minutes. Pour sauce over cannelloni tubes, sprinkle with mozzarella cheese and bake for 40 minutes or until pasta is tender and cheese is golden.

Serves 4

Vegetable Cannelloni

Vegetable and Chilli Pasta

VEGETABLE AND CHILLI PASTA

2 eggplant (aubergines)
salt
500 g/1 lb pasta shells
¹/₄ cup/60 mL/2 fl oz olive oil
2 onions, chopped
2 fresh red chillies, seeded and chopped
2 cloves garlic, crushed
2 x 440 g/14 oz canned tomatoes,
undrained and mashed
¹/₂ cup/125 mL/4 fl oz dry white wine
2 tablespoons chopped fresh basil or
1 teaspoon dried basil

Serves 4

1   Cut eggplant (aubergines) into 2 cm/
³/₄ in cubes. Place in a colander, sprinkle
with salt and set aside to drain for 10
minutes. Rinse eggplant (aubergines)
under cold running water and pat dry.

2   Cook pasta in boiling water in a large
saucepan following packet directions.
Drain, set aside and keep warm.

3   Heat oil in a large frying pan over
a medium heat and cook eggplant
(aubergines) in batches, for 5 minutes
or until golden. Remove eggplant
(aubergines) from pan, drain on
absorbent kitchen paper and set aside.

4   Add onions, chillies and garlic to pan
and cook, stirring, for 3 minutes or until
onions are golden. Stir in tomatoes, wine
and basil, bring to simmering and simmer
for 5 minutes. To serve, spoon sauce over
hot pasta.

The microwave oven has
made reheating pasta not
only easy but successful in a
way that it never was before.
To reheat pasta in the
microwave, place cooked
pasta, with or without sauce
in a covered, microwave-
safe dish and reheat on HIGH
(100%), stirring once or twice
for 2-3 minutes, or until pasta
is hot. The exact length of
time will of course depend
on how much pasta you are
reheating.

PENNE WITH GORGONZOLA SAUCE

500 g/1 lb penne

GORGONZOLA SAUCE
1 cup/250 mL/8 fl oz cream (double)
$^1/_2$ cup/125 mL/4 fl oz vegetable stock
$^1/_2$ cup/125 mL/4 fl oz white wine
125 g/4 oz Gorgonzola or blue cheese,
crumbled
2 tablespoons chopped flat-leaf
parsley
$^1/_2$ teaspoon ground nutmeg
freshly ground black pepper

1   Cook pasta in boiling water in a large saucepan following packet directions. Drain, set aside and keep warm.

2   To make sauce, place cream, stock, wine and Gorgonzola or blue cheese in a saucepan and cook, over a medium heat, stirring constantly, until smooth. Bring to simmering and simmer for 8 minutes or until sauce thickens.

3   Add parsley, nutmeg and black pepper to taste to sauce, bring to simmering and simmer for 2 minutes. Spoon sauce over hot pasta.

Serves 4

Reheating pasta can be done successfully, if it is already combined with a sauce. To reheat, place in a greased ovenproof dish, cover with foil, and reheat in a moderate oven.

Deep-dish Vegetarian Pizza

1 quantity Basic Pizza Dough (page 74)
4 tablespoons tomato paste (purée)
2 teaspoons olive oil
2 cloves garlic, crushed
8 leaves spinach, shredded
125 g/4 oz mixed mushrooms
1 red pepper, chopped
2 tablespoons chopped fresh oregano or
1 teaspoon dried oregano
60 g/2 oz grated Parmesan cheese
freshly ground black pepper

1   Prepare pizza dough as described in recipe, then press into the base and up the sides of a lightly greased 23 cm/9 in springform or sandwich tin to form a 4 cm/1¹/₂ in rim. Spread dough with tomato paste (purée) and set aside.

2   Heat oil in a frying pan over a medium heat. Add garlic and spinach and cook, stirring, for 3 minutes or until spinach wilts. Drain spinach mixture well and spread over dough. Top spinach with mushrooms, red pepper and oregano, then sprinkle with Parmesan cheese and season to taste with black pepper. Bake for 25 minutes or until cheese is golden and base is crisp.

Left: Penne with Gorgonzola Sauce
Below: Deep-dish Vegetarian Pizza

Serves 4

Oven temperature
200°C, 400°F, Gas 6

Fresh Parmesan cheese is available from continental delicatessens and some supermarkets. It is best purchased in a piece then grated as required. Once you have tried fresh Parmesan you will realise that it has a much milder and better flavour than the grated powder that comes in packets.

Flour shaker, seive and board Appley Hoare

SOMETHING SPECIAL

*Pasta is perfect for impromptu entertaining, while pizzas are
great for feeding a crowd. This collection of recipes using more
exotic ingredients shows just how good these foods are for
entertaining. All that is needed to complete your meal is a
tossed salad of mixed lettuces or for a larger gathering a
selection of salads and some crusty bread or rolls.*

SMOKED SALMON PIZZAS

Oven temperature
200°C, 400°F, Gas 6

If lemon thyme is unavailable
you can use ¹/₂ teaspoon
dried thyme and ¹/₂
teaspoon finely grated
lemon rind. Sprinkle the
thyme over the pizza bases
at the beginning of cooking
and sprinkle the lemon rind
over the pizzas just prior to
serving.

1 quantity Basic Pizza Dough (page 74)
1 tablespoon olive oil
200 g/6¹/₂ oz smoked salmon slices
freshly ground black pepper
4 tablespoons crème fraîche or sour
cream
4 teaspoons salmon caviar (optional)
2 tablespoons chopped fresh lemon
thyme

1   Prepare pizza dough as described in
recipe. Divide into four portions and
shape each to form a 15 cm/6 in round.
Place rounds on lightly greased baking
trays, brush with oil and bake for 15
minutes or until crisp and golden.

2   Reduce oven temperature to 180°C/
350°F/Gas 4. Top pizzas with smoked
salmon and black pepper to taste and
bake for 8 minutes or until salmon is hot.

3   Just prior to serving, top pizzas with
crème fraîche or sour cream and caviar (if
using) and sprinkle with thyme.

Serves 4

*Pancetta and Pear Pizzas (page 52),
Smoked Salmon Pizzas*

PANCETTA AND PEAR PIZZAS

Oven temperature
200°C, 400°F, Gas 6

A pizza dough made with olive oil has a crisp exterior and a tender centre. Many professional pizza-makers will also brush the dough with olive oil before topping – this prevents it from drying out and helps ensure a golden colour.

1 quantity Basic Pizza Dough (page 74)
155 g/5 oz pancetta or bacon,
thinly sliced
2 firm pears, cored, peeled and sliced
100 g/3$^{1}/_{2}$ oz creamy blue cheese, such
as Gorgonzola, crumbled
60 g/2 oz walnuts, chopped
125 g/4 oz rocket, roughly chopped
2 tablespoons balsamic or
red wine vinegar
freshly ground black pepper

Serves 4

1   Prepare pizza dough as described in recipe. Divide into four portions and shape each to form a 15 cm/6 round. Place rounds on lightly greased baking trays and cover with pancetta or bacon.

2   Arrange pear slices attractively on top of pancetta or bacon, then sprinkle with cheese and walnuts. Bake for 15-20 minutes or until base is crisp and golden.

3   Just prior to serving, toss rocket with vinegar and pile on top of pizzas. Season to taste with black pepper and serve immediately.

SCALLOP AND RED PEPPER PASTA

What's the easiest way to eat ribbon pasta? Firstly, serve it in a shallow bowl or on a plate with a slight rim. To eat the pasta, slip a few strands on to your fork, then twirl them against the plate, or a spoon, into a ball – the trick is to take only small forkfuls and to wind the pasta tightly so that there are no dangling strands.

500 g/1 lb tagliarini
1 tablespoon olive oil
500 g/1 lb scallops
100 g/3$^{1}/_{2}$ oz prosciutto or lean ham, cut
into thin strips
2 tablespoons lemon juice
2 tablespoons chopped fresh basil or
1 teaspoon dried basil
freshly ground black pepper
1 cup/250 mL/8 fl oz chicken stock
1 red pepper, cut into strips
2 leeks, cut into strips

GREMOLATA
3 cloves garlic, crushed
$^{1}/_{2}$ bunch flat-leaf parsley, leaves
finely chopped
1 tablespoon finely grated lemon rind

Serves 4

1   To make Gremolata, place garlic, parsley and lemon rind in a bowl and mix well to combine.

2   Cook pasta in boiling water in a large saucepan following packet directions. Drain, set aside and keep warm.

3   Heat oil in a frying pan over a medium heat. Add scallops and prosciutto or ham and cook, stirring, for 3 minutes or until scallops just turn opaque and prosciutto or ham is crisp. Remove pan from heat, stir in lemon juice, basil and black pepper to taste and set aside.

4   Place stock in a saucepan, bring to simmering and simmer until reduced by half. Add red pepper and leeks and simmer for 3 minutes. Add pasta and scallop mixture to stock mixture. Toss to combine and top with Gremolata.

Scallop and Red Pepper Pasta,
Spaghetti with Tuna and Cress

SPAGHETTI WITH TUNA AND CRESS

500 g/1 lb spaghetti
500 g/1 lb tuna steaks, thinly sliced
1 bunch/250 g/8 oz watercress, leaves removed and stems discarded
125 g/4 oz black olives
1 tablespoon finely grated lime rind
2 teaspoons finely grated fresh ginger
$^1/_4$ cup/60 mL/2 fl oz balsamic or red wine vinegar
1 tablespoon olive oil
2 tablespoons lime juice

1   Cook pasta in boiling water in a large saucepan of boiling water following packet directions. Drain well and place in a large serving bowl.

2   Add tuna, watercress, olives, lime rind, ginger, vinegar, oil and lime juice to hot pasta and toss to combine. Serve immediately.

Serves 4

The tuna in this dish is not cooked before adding to the pasta, however you will find because it is thinly sliced the heat of the pasta will cook it. Drained canned tuna can be used if you wish.

LOBSTER IN PASTA NETS

375 g/12 oz angel's hair pasta
3 uncooked lobster tails, shelled and
flesh cut into 4 cm/1¹/₂ in pieces
flour
vegetable oil for deep frying

LIME CREAM
¹/₂ cup/125 g/4 oz mayonnaise
¹/₄ cup/60 g/2 oz sour cream
1 tablespoon finely grated lime rind
1 tablespoon lime juice
1 tablespoon wholegrain mustard
2 tablespoons chopped fresh tarragon or
1 teaspoon dried tarragon

1   Cook pasta in boiling water in a large
saucepan until almost cooked. Drain,
rinse under cold running water, drain
again and pat dry on absorbent kitchen
paper. Set aside.

2   To make Lime Cream, place
mayonnaise, sour cream, lime rind, lime
juice, mustard and tarragon in a bowl and
mix to combine. Set aside.

3   Dust lobster pieces with flour. Wrap a
few stands of pasta around each lobster
piece. Continue wrapping with pasta to
form a net effect around lobster.

4   Heat oil in a large saucepan until a
cube of bread dropped in browns in 50
seconds. Cook pasta wrapped lobster in
batches for 2-3 minutes or until golden.
Drain on absorbent kitchen paper and
serve immediately with Lime Cream.

Serves 4

This dish is also delicious
made with large uncooked
prawns.

TORTELLINI WITH ONION CONFIT

1¹/₂ cups/375 mL/12 fl oz beef stock
750 g/1¹/₂ lb beef or veal tortellini
250 g/8 oz small peas
2 tablespoons chopped fresh tarragon or
1 teaspoon dried tarragon

ONION CONFIT
30 g/1 oz butter
2 onions, thinly sliced
2 teaspoons sugar
1 tablespoon chopped fresh thyme or
¹/₂ teaspoon dried thyme
1 cup/250 mL/8 fl oz red wine
2 tablespoons red wine vinegar

1   To make confit, melt butter in a saucepan over a medium heat, add onions and cook, stirring, for 3 minutes or until onions are soft. Stir in sugar and cook for 2 minutes longer. Add thyme, wine and vinegar, bring to simmering and simmer, stirring frequently, for 40 minutes or until mixture reduces and thickens.

2   Place stock in a saucepan, bring to the boil and boil until reduced by half. Keep warm.

3   Cook pasta in boiling water in a large saucepan following packet directions. Drain well. Add pasta, confit, peas and tarragon to stock, bring to simmering and simmer for 2-3 minutes or until peas are just cooked.

Serves 4

Serve this unusual pasta dish with a sautée of mixed green vegetables and crusty bread or rolls.

TAGLIATELLE SOUFFLE

Left: Tortellini with Onion Confit
Above: Tagliatelle Soufflé

375 g/12 oz tagliatelle
60 g/2 oz butter
$^1/_4$ cup/30 g/1 oz flour
$1^1/_2$ cups/375 mL/12 fl oz milk
75 g/$2^1/_2$ oz Gruyére cheese, grated
4 egg yolks, lightly beaten
200 g/$6^1/_2$ oz smoked ham, cut
into strips
freshly ground black pepper
7 egg whites

1   Cook pasta in boiling water in a large saucepan following packet directions. Drain and set aside.

2   Melt butter in a saucepan over a medium heat, add flour and cook, stirring, for 1 minute. Remove pan from heat and whisk in milk. Return pan to heat and cook, stirring constantly, for 4-5 minutes or until sauce boils and thickens. Set aside to cool slightly.

3   Stir cheese, egg yolks, ham, black pepper to taste and pasta into sauce.

4   Place egg whites in a bowl and beat until stiff peaks form. Fold egg white mixture into pasta mixture and pour into a greased 1 litre/$1^3/_4$ pt capacity soufflé dish and bake for 25-30 minutes or until soufflé is puffed and golden.

Serves 4

Oven temperature
200°C, 400°F, Gas 6

This soufflé is an interesting and different dish to serve for a special brunch or breakfast.

THAI BEEF PIZZAS

Oven temperature
200°C, 400°F, Gas 6

500 g/1 lb rump steak, trimmed of all
visible fat
2 quantities Basic Pizza
Dough (page 74)
3 tablespoons tomato purée
2 tablespoons sweet chilli sauce
3 spring onions, chopped
1 carrot, cut into matchsticks
2 stalks celery, cut into matchsticks

THAI MARINADE
1 clove garlic, crushed
3 tablespoons soy sauce
1 stalk fresh lemon grass, chopped or
1 teaspoon dried lemon grass or
1 teaspoon finely grated lemon rind
3 tablespoons chopped fresh coriander

Combining two popular
cuisines this pizza is ideal to
serve when you can't decide
whether to choose Oriental
or Mediterranean.

1 To make marinade, place garlic, soy
sauce, lemon grass and coriander in a large
bowl and mix to combine. Set aside.

2 Heat a nonstick frying pan over a high
heat, add steak and cook for 1 minute
each side. Remove steak from pan and
slice thinly. Add steak to marinade, cover
and set aside to marinate for 15 minutes.

3 Prepare pizza dough as described in
recipe. Shape dough into two 30 cm/12 in
rounds or two 15 x25 cm/6 x10 in
rectangles and place on lightly greased
baking trays.

4 Combine tomato purée and chilli
sauce, spread over pizza bases and bake for
15 minutes.

5 Top pizza bases with spring onions,
carrot and celery, then arrange beef slices
attractively on top and bake for 10
minutes longer or until topping is heated
through and base is crisp and golden.

Serves 8

58

PROSCIUTTO AND FIG PIZZAS

1 quantity Basic Pizza Dough (page 74)
2 teaspoons olive oil
125 g/4 oz prosciutto
4 fresh or dried figs, sliced
60 g/2 oz pine nuts
1 tablespoon chopped fresh rosemary or
$^1/_2$ teaspoon dried rosemary
freshly ground black pepper

1 Prepare pizza dough as described in recipe. Divide dough into four portions and shape each to form a 15 cm/6 in round. Place rounds on lightly greased baking trays.

2 Brush dough with oil and top with prosciutto and fig slices. Sprinkle with pine nuts, rosemary and black pepper to taste and bake for 15 minutes or until bases are crisp and golden.

Oven temperature
190°C, 375°F, Gas 5

Perfect for an autumn luncheon when fresh figs are in season and at their best. For a complete meal accompany with garlic bread, a salad and a glass of dry white wine.

Left: Thai Beef Pizzas
Below: Prosciutto and Fig Pizzas

Serves 4

Board Appley Hoare

Smoked Chicken Pappardelle

750 g/1 1/2 lb pappardelle
1.5 kg/3 lb smoked chicken, skin
removed and flesh sliced
1/2 cup/125 mL/4 fl oz white wine
1 cup/250 mL/8 fl oz cream
2 tablespoons snipped fresh chives
freshly ground black pepper

NASTURTIUM BUTTER
125 g/4 oz butter, softened
1 clove garlic, crushed
1 tablespoon lime juice
6 nasturtium flowers, finely chopped

The perfect accompaniment
to this dish is a salad of
watercress or rocket tossed
in balsamic vinegar and
topped with shavings of
Parmesan cheese.
The Nasturtium Butter is also
delicious as a sandwich
filling when teamed with
watercress or rocket.

1   To make Nasturtium Butter, place butter, garlic, lime juice and flowers in a bowl, mix well to combine and set aside.

2   Cook pasta in boiling water in a large saucepan following packet directions. Drain, set aside and keep warm.

3   Heat a nonstick frying pan over a medium heat, add chicken and cook, stirring, for 1 minute. Add wine, cream, chives and black pepper to taste, bring to simmering and simmer for 2 minutes. To serve, top pasta with chicken mixture and Nasturtium Butter.

Serves 6

Plate Pillivuyt

Left: Smoked Chicken Pappardelle
Above: Raspberry Salmon Pasta

RASPBERRY SALMON PASTA

500 g/1 lb pepper or plain fettuccine
1 tablespoon vegetable oil
500 g/1 lb salmon fillet, bones and skin removed
2 tablespoons lemon juice
2 tablespoons chopped fresh dill

RASPBERRY MAYONNAISE
200 g/6¹/₂ oz raspberries
1 cup/250 g/8 oz low-oil mayonnaise
2 teaspoons wholegrain mustard
1 tablespoon lemon juice

1 To make mayonnaise, place raspberries in a food processor or blender and process until smooth. Push purée through a fine sieve and discard seeds. Add mayonnaise, mustard and lemon juice to purée, mix to combine and set aside.

2 Cook pasta in boiling water in a large saucepan following packet directions. Drain, set aside and keep warm.

3 Heat oil in a frying or grill pan over a medium heat. Brush salmon with lemon juice and sprinkle with dill. Place salmon in pan and cook for 2-3 minutes each side or until flesh flakes when tested with a fork. Remove salmon from pan and cut into thick slices.

4 To serve, divide pasta between six serving plates. Top with salmon slices and drizzle with raspberry mayonnaise. Serve immediately.

Serves 6

This pretty dish looks great served with a salad of red and green lettuces.

PIZZA PARTY

Pizzas, salads and thickshakes – what better way to entertain a group of teenagers. This menu will satifsfy ten hungry teenagers and includes a selection of pizzas, two salads and a thickshake to create a pizza party that your teenagers will ask you to repeat time and again.

MENU

Peperoni Pizzas

Satay Chicken Pizzas

Cheese Calzone

Green Salad with
Creamy Dressing

Carrot and Sultana
Salad

Choc-malt
Thickshakes

Oven temperature
200°C, 400°F, Gas 6

A pizza party can be a great way to entertain a group of young people and to get them involved with cooking. As the dough needs some time to rise it is a good idea to prepare it in advance (or use purchased pizza bases). At the time of the party lay out the ingredients for topping the pizzas and allow the guests to shape and top their own pizzas – you may be surprised at some of the combinations.

PEPERONI PIZZAS

2 quantities Basic Pizza
Dough (page 74)
$^3/_4$ cup/185 mL/6 fl oz tomato paste
(purée)
20 slices peperoni
20 slices cabanossi (kabanos)
200 g/6$^1/_2$ oz button mushrooms, sliced
1 green pepper, chopped
250 g/8 oz mozzarella cheese, grated

1 Prepare pizza dough as described in recipe, then shape into two 30 cm/12 in rounds and place on lightly greased baking trays. Spread with tomato paste (purée), then top each base with half the peperoni and cabanossi (kabanos).

2 Arrange half the mushrooms and green pepper on each pizza and sprinkle each with half the mozzarella cheese. Bake for 25-30 minutes or until cheese is golden and base is crisp.

Serves 10

*Peperoni Pizza,
Green Salad with Creamy Dressing (page 64),
Choc-malt Thickshake (page 65)*

Green Salad with Creamy Dressing

6 rashers bacon, chopped
2 lettuces of your choice, leaves
separated and torn into pieces
250 g/8 oz cherry tomatoes, halved
2 carrots, cut into strips
2 sticks celery, cut into strips
125 g/4 oz snow peas (mangetout)

CREAMY DRESSING
$^1/_2$ cup/125 g/4 oz mayonnaise
$^1/_2$ cup/125 g/4 oz sour cream
1 tablespoon lemon juice
freshly ground black pepper

1   Cook bacon in a frying pan over a medium heat for 4-5 minutes or until crisp. Remove bacon from pan and drain on absorbent kitchen paper until cool.

2   Arrange lettuces, tomatoes, carrots, celery, snow peas (mangetout) and bacon on a serving platter or in a large salad bowl.

3   To make dressing, place mayonnaise, sour cream, lemon juice and black pepper to taste in a bowl and mix to combine. Drizzle dressing over salad, cover and chill until required.

Serves 10

If you do not have time to make a yeast based dough for your pizza a scone dough is a good alternative. See page 72 for Scone Dough recipe.

Satay Chicken Pizzas

2 quantities Basic Pizza
Dough (page 74)
1 cup/250 mL/8 fl oz satay sauce
1 red pepper, sliced
1 green pepper, sliced
1 carrot, cut into thin strips
100 g/3$^1/_2$ oz bean sprouts
1 cooked chicken, flesh cut into
small pieces
185 g/6 oz tasty cheese (mature
Cheddar), grated

1   Prepare pizza dough as described in recipe, then shape into two 30 cm/12 in rounds and place on lightly greased baking trays.

2   Spread dough with satay sauce. Arrange half the red pepper, green pepper, carrot and bean sprouts on each pizza base. Top each base with half the chicken and sprinkle each with half the cheese. Bake for 20-25 minutes or until cheese is golden and base is crisp.

Serves 10

Oven temperature
200°C, 400°F, Gas 6

This is a great way to use up leftover roast chicken. This pizza is also delicious made with cold roast beef, lamb or turkey. If you only want to make one pizza simply halve the ingredients.

Satay Chicken Pizzas

Choc-Malt Thickshakes

4 tablespoons drinking chocolate
4 tablespoons malted milk powder
1 litre/1³/₄ pt chocolate or
vanilla ice cream
1 cup/250 mL/8 fl oz cold milk

Place drinking chocolate, milk powder, ice cream and milk in a food processor or blender and process until smooth. Pour into glasses and serve immediately.

Makes 4 thickshakes

Oven temperature
200°C, 400°F, Gas 6

These crisp parcels contain a rich smooth cheese filling. Blue cheese lovers will enjoy these calzone made with blue cheese in place of the Swiss cheese.

CHEESE CALZONE

2 quantities Basic Pizza
Dough (page 74)
olive oil

CHEESE FILLING
200 g/6$^{1}/_{2}$ oz ricotta cheese, drained
60 g/2 oz tasty cheese (mature
Cheddar), grated
60 g/2 oz Swiss cheese, grated
60 g/2 oz mozzarella cheese, grated
3 tablespoons snipped fresh chives
freshly ground ground pepper

1   To make filling, place ricotta cheese, tasty cheese (mature Cheddar), Swiss cheese, mozzarella cheese, chives and black pepper to taste in a bowl and mix to combine. Set aside.

2   Prepare pizza dough as described in recipe and divide into 10 portions. Shape each portion into a 5 mm/$^{1}/_{4}$ in thick round with a 15 cm/6 in diameter.

3   Place spoonfuls of filling in the centre of each round, brush edges with water, then fold over to form a half circle. Press edges together to seal and using a fork make a decorative pattern. Brush calzone with olive oil, place on lightly greased baking trays and bake for 15 minutes or until puffed and golden.

Makes 10

CARROT AND SULTANA SALAD

6 carrots, grated
125 g/4 oz sultanas
60 g/2 oz chopped nuts

ORANGE DRESSING
$^{1}/_{4}$ cup/60 mL/2 fl oz orange juice
2 tablespoons honey

1   Place carrots and sultanas in a serving bowl.

2   To make dressing, place orange juice and honey in a small bowl and whisk to combine. Spoon dressing over carrot mixture and toss to combine. Sprinkle with nuts, cover and refrigerate until required.

Serves 10

Cheese Calzone, Carrot and Sultana Salad

PASTA PARTY

This easy pasta party for eight is sure to delight your friends. Much of the preparation can be done in advance leaving you free to enjoy your guests. For a complete meal offer an antipasto platter to start, serve the pasta with a selection of salads and breads and finish with seasonal fresh fruit.

MENU
Antipasto Platter

Cajun Chicken
Fettuccine
Cannelloni with Pesto
Cream
Pasta Salad with
Roasted Garlic
Selection of salads
Selection of breads

Selection seasonal
fresh fruit

If planning ahead the salsa can be prepared up to a day in advance. The chicken can be prepared and tossed in the spice mixture several hours in advance, leaving only the cooking of the chicken and pasta to do at the last minute.

CAJUN CHICKEN FETTUCCINE

2 tablespoons sweet paprika
2 cloves garlic, crushed
2 teaspoons crushed black peppercorns
1 tablespoon ground cumin
1 tablespoon ground coriander
$^{1}/_{2}$ teaspoon chilli powder
6 boneless chicken breast fillets, sliced
2 teaspoons vegetable oil
750 g/1 $^{1}/_{2}$ lb fettuccine

TOMATO SALSA
6 ripe tomatoes, chopped
2 fresh red chillies, seeded and finely chopped
1 green pepper, chopped
1 tablespoon brown sugar
3 tablespoons balsamic or red wine vinegar

1   To make salsa, place tomatoes, chillies, green pepper, sugar and vinegar in a bowl and toss to combine. Set aside.

2   Place paprika, garlic, black peppercorns, cumin, coriander and chilli powder in a bowl and mix to combine. Add chicken and toss to coat with spice mixture. Heat oil in a frying pan over a medium heat, add chicken and cook, stirring, for 5 minutes or until chicken is tender. Remove chicken from pan, set aside and keep warm.

3   Cook pasta in boiling water in a large saucepan following packet directions. Drain well and place in a serving dish. Add chicken, toss to combine and serve with salsa.

Serves 8

Cajun Chicken Fettuccine

CANNELLONI WITH PESTO CREAM

Oven temperature
180°C, 350°F, Gas 4

16 sheets fresh spinach lasagne

SPINACH FILLING
2 teaspoons olive oil
1 onion, chopped
2 cloves garlic, crushed
12 leaves spinach, shredded
250 g/8 oz button mushrooms, finely chopped
1 cup/250 mL/8 fl oz tomato purée

PESTO CREAM
³/₄ cup/185 g/6 oz ready-made pesto
300 g/9¹/₂ oz sour cream
1 cup/200 g/6¹/₂ oz natural yogurt
freshly ground black pepper

This dish can be prepared up to a day in advance. Cover and store in the refrigerator until ready to bake.

1   To make filling, heat oil in a frying pan over a medium heat, add onion and garlic and cook, stirring, for 3 minutes or until onion is soft. Add spinach and mushrooms and cook for 4 minutes

longer. Stir in tomato purée, bring to simmering and simmer, stirring occasionally, for 10-15 minutes or until liquid evaporates.

2   To make Pesto Cream, place pesto, sour cream, yogurt and black pepper to taste in a bowl and mix to combine.

3   Cook lasagne sheets in boiling water in a large saucepan following packet directions. Drain well.

4   Place spoonfuls of filling along one long edge of each lasagne sheet and roll up. Place rolls join side down in a greased ovenproof dish and spoon over Pesto Cream. Bake for 25-30 minutes or until hot and bubbling.

Serves 8

PASTA SALAD WITH ROASTED GARLIC

Oven temperature
180°C, 350°F, Gas 4

20 cloves unpeeled garlic
8 rashers bacon, chopped
30 g/1 oz butter
2 cups/125 g/4 oz breadcrumbs, made from stale bread
4 tablespoons chopped fresh mixed herb leaves
freshly ground black pepper
750 g/1¹/₂ lb spinach, tomato or plain linguine

The garlic can be roasted and the bacon and breadcrumb mixture cooked several hours in advance, leaving just the cooking of the pasta and the final assembly of the salad to do at the last minute.

1   Place unpeeled garlic cloves on a lightly greased baking tray and bake for 10-12 minutes or until soft and golden. Peel garlic and set aside.

2   Cook bacon in a frying pan over a medium heat for 4-5 minutes or until crisp. Drain on absorbent kitchen paper.

3   Melt butter in a clean frying pan, add breadcrumbs, herbs and black pepper to taste and cook, stirring for 4-5 minutes or until breadcrumbs are golden.

4   Cook pasta in boiling water in a large saucepan following packet directions. Drain well and place in a warm serving bowl. Add garlic, bacon and breadcrumb mixture, toss and serve immediately.

Serves 8

*Pasta Salad with Roasted Garlic,
Cannelloni with Pesto Cream*

Board Appley Hoare White bowls Pillivuyt

THE BASICS

A pizza dough, a guide to cooking perfect pasta and some interesting pizza base alternatives are just some of the tips you will find in this chapter. For easy reference the secrets of cooking and preparing delicious pizzas and tasty pasta dishes have been collected together in one place.

SCONE DOUGH

Oven temperature
220°C, 425°F, Gas 7

A scone dough is a good alternative to using a yeast based dough when time is short. Follow the instructions in the pizza recipe for topping. The cooking time will usually be a little less when using a scone dough.

2 cups/250 g/8 oz self-raising flour
1 teaspoon baking powder
2 teaspoons sugar
60 g/2 oz butter, chopped
1 egg, lightly beaten
$^1/_2$ cup/125 mL/4 fl oz milk

1 Sift flour and baking powder together into a bowl, add sugar. Using your fingertips, rub in butter until mixture resembles fine breadcrumbs.

2 Make a well in the centre of flour mixture and using a round-ended knife, mix in egg and enough milk to form a soft dough.

3 Turn dough onto a lightly floured surface and knead with fingertips until smooth. Using heel of hand, press dough out evenly, shape and top as desired, then bake for 15-20 minutes or until base is cooked and golden.

ALTERNATIVE PIZZA BASES

Next time you are in the supermarket have a look in the bread and freezer sections and see what would be suitable to use as an easy alternative to making your own pizza base.

Focaccia bread

Vaccum-packed pizza bases

Frozen pizza bases

Pitta bread rounds

Large hamburger buns – split and use to make individual pizzas

Muffins – split and use to make individual pizzas – children love them

Remember that choosing one of these as your base may affect the cooking time of your pizza. If using already cooked breads and pitta bread, the cooking will only take 10-15 minutes – just long enough to heat the top and base.

Check the bread and freezer sections for alternative pizza base ideas

BASIC PIZZA DOUGH

1 teaspoon active dry yeast
pinch sugar
²/₃ cup/170 mL/5¹/₂ fl oz warm water
2 cups/250 mL/8 oz flour
¹/₂ teaspoon salt
¹/₄ cup/60 mL/2 fl oz olive oil

This pizza dough has been used throughout this book.

1   Place yeast, sugar and water in a large bowl and mix to dissolve. Set aside in a warm, draught-free place for 5 minutes or until foamy.

2   Place flour and salt in a food processor and pulse once or twice to sift. With machine running, slowly pour in oil and yeast mixture and process to form a rough dough. Turn dough onto a lightly floured surface and knead for 5 minutes or until soft and shiny. Add more flour if necessary.

3   Lightly oil a large bowl, then roll dough around in it to cover the surface with oil. Cover bowl tightly with plastic food wrap and place in a warm, draught-free place for 1¹/₂-2 hours or until dough has doubled in volume. Knock down and remove dough from bowl. Knead briefly before using as desired.

Makes 250 g/8 oz dough

VARIATIONS

Ring the changes by adding or substituting ingredients in the Basic Pizza Dough.

HERB PIZZA DOUGH: Add 1 teaspoon dried mixed herbs to the flour mixture.

CHEESE PIZZA DOUGH: Add 60 g/ 2 oz grated tasty cheese (mature Cheddar) to the flour mixture.

TOMATO PIZZA DOUGH: Replace the water with ²/₃ cup/170 mL/5¹/₂ fl oz tomato juice – you will need to warm the tomato juice.

WHOLEMEAL PIZZA DOUGH: Replace half the flour with wholemeal flour. You may need to add a little extra water.

Homemade pizza dough is a tasty and economical alternative to purchased pizza bases

KNOW YOUR PASTA

If a suffix is added it indicates:
-ini, a smaller version
-oni, a larger version
-rigate, ridged; and
-lisce, smooth.

Angel's hair pasta: Also labelled as *capelli di angelo* this is an extremely long thin pasta, that is dried in coils to prevent it from breaking. Because of its delicate nature angel's hair pasta is best served with a light sauce.

Cannelloni: This large hollow pasta is most often stuffed, topped with a sauce and cheese, then baked. Cannelloni can also be stuffed and deep-fried until crisp. If deep-frying, the tubes will need to be boiled before stuffing and frying. Lasagne sheets can also be used for baked cannelloni – spread the filling down the centre of the pasta then roll up.

Farfalle: Meaning 'butterflies', this bow-shaped pasta is ideal for serving with meat and vegetable sauces, as the sauce becomes trapped in the folds.

Fettuccine: A flat ribbon pasta that is used in a similar way to spaghetti. Often sold coiled in nests, fettuccine is particularly good with creamy sauces, which cling better than heavier sauces.

Lasagne: These flat sheets of pasta are most often layered with a meat, fish or vegetable sauce, topped with cheese, then baked to make a delicious and satisfying dish. Instant (no precooking required) lasagne that you do not have to cook before using is also available.

Linguine: This long thin pasta looks somewhat like spaghetti but has square-cut ends. It can be used in the same way as spaghetti, fettuccine and tagliatelle.

Macaroni: Short-cut or 'elbow' macaroni, very common outside of Italy, is most often used in baked dishes and in the ever-popular macaroni cheese.

Orecchiette: Its name means 'little ears' and this is exactly what this pasta looks like. It is made without eggs and tends to have a chewier and firmer texture than some other pastas. Traditionally a homemade pasta, it can now be purchased dried from Italian food stores and some supermarkets.

Pappardelle: This very wide ribbon pasta was traditionally served with a sauce made of hare, herbs and wine, but today it is teamed with any rich sauce.

Penne: A short tubular pasta, similar to macaroni, but with ends cut at an angle rather than straight. It is particularly suited to being served with meat and heavier sauces, which catch in the hollows.

Shell pasta: Also called conchiglie, if large, or conchigliette, if smaller. The large shells are ideal for stuffing and a fish filling is often favoured because of the shape of the pasta. Small shells are popular in casseroles, soups and salads.

Spaghetti: Deriving its name from the Italian word *spago* meaning 'string', spaghetti is the most popular and best known of all pastas outside of Italy. It can be simply served with butter or oil and is good with almost any sauce.

Spiral pasta: Also called fusilli, this pasta is great served with substantial meat sauces, as the sauce becomes trapped in the coils or twists.

Tagliarini: Similar to fettuccine, this is the name often given to homemade fettuccine.

Tagliatelle: Another of the flat ribbon pastas, tagliatelle is eaten more in northern Italy than in the south and is used in the same ways as fettuccine.

There are some general rules that will ensure that you enjoy your pasta to the fullest: thin, long pasta needs a good clinging sauce; hollow or twisted shapes take chunky sauces; wide, flat noodles carry rich sauces; and delicate shapes require a light sauce without large pieces in it.

COOKING PASTA

Cook pasta in a large, deep saucepan of water: the general rule is 4 cups/1 litre/1 $^3/_4$ pt water to 100 g/3$^1/_2$ oz pasta. Bring the water to a rolling boil, toss in salt to taste (in Italy, 1 tablespoon per every 100 g/3$^1/_2$ oz is usual), then stir in pasta. If you wish, add some oil.

When the water comes back to the boil, begin timing. The pasta is done when it is 'al dente', that is tender but with resistance to the bite. Remove the pasta from the water by straining through a colander or lifting out of the saucepan with tongs or a fork.

HOW MUCH PASTA TO SERVE

PASTA TYPE	FIRST COURSE	MAIN MEAL
Dried Pasta	60-75 g 2-2$^1/_2$ oz	75-100 g 2$^1/_2$-3$^1/_2$ oz
Fresh Pasta	75-100 g 2$^1/_2$-3$^1/_2$ oz	125-155 g 4-5 oz
Filled Pasta	155-185 g 5-6 oz	185-200 g 6-6$^1/_2$ oz

You will find that the pasta quantities used in this book are fairly generous. In many cases, all you will need to make a complete meal is a tossed green or vegetable salad and some crusty bread or rolls.

INDEX